Article I.   Universal Arian Creed 4

Article II.   The Inspired Word of God 11

Section 1.01   A. Romans 12:22 11

Article III.   There is but One Living and True God 13

Article IV.   God Created All Things 16

Article V.   In the divinity of the Lord Jesus Christ 21

Article VI.   In the Sinfulness of Man 27

Article VII.   In the Salvation of Man 30

Article VIII.   In the Sanctification of the Believer 33

Article IX.   In the Baptism of the Holy Spirit 36

Article X.   In the Church and its Mission 39

Article XI.   In the Ordinances of the Church 43

Article XII.   In Divine Healing: 45

Article XIII.   In the Second Coming of Christ 48

Article XIV.   In the Final Judgment 55

Article XV.   In the Final Judgment p2 58

Article XVI.   In a New Heaven and a New Earth 59

Article XVII. II. Events of New Heaven and Earth 61

Article I. Universal Arian Creed

Ἡ μὲν γὰρ ἐκκλησία, καίπερ καθ' ὅλης τῆς οἰκουμένης ἕως περάτων τῆς γῆς διεσπαρμένη, παρὰ δὲ τῶν Ἀποστόλων καὶ τῶν ἐκείνων μαθητῶν παραλαβοῦσα τὴν [πίστιν]

The Church, though scattered through the whole world to the ends of the earth, has received from the Apostles and their disciples the faith

Πιστεύομεν εἰς ἕνα θεόν πατέρα παντοκράτορα,

We believe in one God the Father Almighty,

τὸν τῶν ἁπάντων ὁρατῶν τε καὶ ἀοράτων ποιητήν·

Maker of all things visible and invisible;

Καὶ εἰς ἕνα κύριον Ἰησοῦν Χριστόν,

And in one Lord Jesus Christ,

τὸν τοῦ θεοῦ λόγον,

the Logos of God,

φῶς ἐκ φωτὸς,

Light of Light,

ζωὴν ἐκ ζωῆς,

Life of Life,

υἱὸν μονογενῆ,

the only-born Son,

πρωτότοκον πάσης κτίσεως,

the first-born of every creature,

πρὸ πάντων τῶν αἰώνων ἐκ τοῦ θεοῦ πατρὸς γεγεννημένον,

begotten of God the Father before all ages,

δἰ οὗ καὶ ἐγένετο τὰ πάντα·

by whom also all things were made;

τὸν διὰ τὴν ἡμετέραν σωτηρίαν σαρκωθέντα καὶ ἐν ἀνθρώποις πολιτευσάμενον,

who for our salvation was made flesh and made his home among men;

καὶ παθόντα,

and suffered;

καὶ ἀναστάντα τῇ τρίτῃ ἡμέρᾳ,

and rose on the third day;

καὶ ἀνελθόντα πρὸς τὸν πατέρα,

and ascended to the Father;

καὶ ἥξοντα πάλιν ἐν δόξῃ κρῖναι ζῶντας καὶ νεκρούς.

and will come again in glory, to judge the quick and the dead.

[Πιστεύομεν] καὶ εἰς ἓν πνεῦμα ἅγιον.

[We believe] also in one Holy Ghost.

Καὶ εἰς ἓν βάπτισμα μετανοίας εἰς ἄφεσιν ἁμαρτιῶν,

And in one baptism of repentance for the remission of sins;

καὶ εἰς μίαν ἁγίαν καθολικὴν ἐκκλησίαν,

and in one holy Universal (Arian) Church;

καὶ εἰς σαρκὸς ἀνάστασιν,

and in the resurrection of the flesh,

καὶ εἰς ζωὴν αἰώνιον.

and in life everlasting.

Τούτων ἕκαστον εἶναι καὶ ὑπάρχειν πιστεύοντες, πατέρα ἀληθῶς πατέρα καὶ υἱὸν ἀληθῶς υἱὸν καὶ πνεῦμα ἅγιον ἀληθῶς πνεῦμα ἅγιον, καθὼς καὶ ὁ κύριος ἡμῶν ἀποστέλλων εἰς τὸ κήρυγμα τοὺς ἑαυτοῦ μαθητὰς εἶπε· πορευθέντες μαθητεύσατε πάντα τὰ ἔθνη, βαπτίζοντες αὐτοὺς εἰς τὸ ὄνομα τοῦ πατρὸς καὶ τοῦ υἱοῦ καὶ τοῦ ἁγίου πνεύματος.

We believe that each of these is and exists, the Father truly Father, and the Son truly Son, and the Holy Ghost truly Holy Ghost; even as our Lord when sending forth his disciples to preach, said: 'Go and make disciples of all nations, baptizing them into the name of the Father, and of the Son, and of the Holy Ghost.'

'And concerning these things we affirm that we so hold and so think, and have of old so held, and will so hold till death, and stand steadfast in this faith, anathematizing all ungodly heresy. We testify before Almighty God the Only True GOD, and our Lord Jesus Christ that we believe all this in heart and soul, and we now so think and speak in truth, being able to show by scriptural evidence and to convince you that we in past times so believed and preached accordingly.

Having then this faith (from the beginning of the Church and holding it to the end) before God and Christ we anathematize all heretical false doctrine. And if any one, contrary to the right faith of the Scriptures, says the one God of the law and the prophets, but denies Christ to be the Son of God, he is a liar, even as also is his father the devil, and is a Jew falsely so called, being possessed of mere carnal circumcision. If any one confesses Christ Jesus the Lord, but denies the God of the law and of the prophets, saying that the Father of Christ is not the Maker of heaven and earth, he has not continued in the truth any more than his father the devil, and is a disciple of Simon Magus, not of the Holy Spirit. If any one says there is one God, and also confesses Christ Jesus, but thinks the Lord to be a mere man, and not the only-begotten God, and Wisdom, and the Word of God, and deems Him to consist merely of a soul and body, such an one is a serpent, that preaches deceit and error for the destruction of men. And such a man is poor in understanding, even as by name he is an Ebionite, and so also he who says that the Son is; the Archangel Michael and/or consubstantial with the Father and the Spirit a Trinity "three whos in one what" , Unbegotten, Uncreated, the Almighty, let him be accursed. Trinitarianism, Gnosticism, Socinianism or circumcision for the gentile let them be accursed. And if he denies Christ a creation and existence as a living person at the beginning but is a thought only before the world was let him be accursed. Teaching not as the divine Scriptures have handed down as each of the true forenamed creedal statements; and if a man teaches or preaches any thing else contrary to what we have received, let him be accursed.

Ἡμεῖς γὰρ πᾶσι τοῖς ἐκ τῶν θείων γραφῶν παραδεδομένοις ὑπό τε τῶν προφητῶν καὶ ἀποστόλων ἀληθινῶς καὶ ἐμφόβως καὶ πιστεύομεν καὶ ἀκολουθοῦμεν.

For we truly and clearly both believe and follow all things from the holy Scriptures that have been transmitted to us by the Prophets and Apostles.

This is the Universal Arian faith; which every man should believe truly and firmly.

Copyright © 2016 by The Kingdom of God and Christ
All rights reserved. This book or any portion thereof
may not be reproduced or used in any manner whatsoever
without the express written permission of the publisher
except for the use of brief quotations in a book review.

Printed in the United States of America

First Printing, 2016

ISBN-13: 978-1539405818

ArianismToday.com

WE BELIEVE...

Article II. The Inspired Word of God

Section 1.01 A. Romans 12:22

(a) And do not be conformed to this world, but be transformed by the renewing of your mind, that you may prove what the will of God is, that which is good and acceptable and perfect. (Rom 12:2 NAS)

- (i) The Word of God is what cleanses our minds.
- (ii) At the same time it is removing ungodly thoughts, it is putting in Godly thoughts.

Section 2.02 B. Psalm 119:105

(a) 105 Thy word is a lamp to my feet, And a light to my path. (Psa 119:105 NAS)

- (i) 1. The Word of God will continue to guide us in His marvelous light.

Section 2.03 C. Ephesians 6:17

(a) 17 And take the helmet of salvation, and the sword of the Spirit, which is the word of God. (Eph 6:17 NAS)

- (i) The Word of God is the only offensive weapon that God has given us to fight off the devil.
- (ii) We need to know the Word of God and how to use it.

Section 2.04 D. Hebrews 4:12

(a) 12 For the word of God is living and active and sharper than any two-edged sword, and piercing as far as the division of soul and spirit, of both joints and marrow, and able to judge the thoughts and intentions of the heart. (Heb 4:12 NAS)

- (i) The Word of God exposes us.
- (ii) There is no part of man that the Word of God cannot penetrate.

Section 2.05 E. James 1:22

(a) 22 But prove yourselves doers of the word, and not merely hearers who delude themselves. (Jam 1:22 NAS)

- (i) Being hearers is not enough we must be doers of the Word.
- (ii) We must apply the Word of God to our lives.

Section 2.06 F. Matthew 7:25

(a) 25 "And the rain descended, and the floods came, and the winds blew, and burst against that house; and yet it did not fall, for it had been founded upon the rock. (Mat 7:25 NAS)

- (i) We need to build our foundation upon the Word of God
    1) THE WORD OF GOD WILL NEVER LET US DOWN.

Section 2.07 G. 2 Timothy 3:15

(a) and that from childhood you have known the sacred writings which are able to give you the wisdom that leads to salvation through faith which is in Christ Jesus. (2Ti 3:15 NAS)

- (i) The Bible has God's stamp of authority on it.
- (ii) It is verbally inspired.
- (iii) This is why we believe it.

Section 2.08 H. Isaiah 43:8

(a) 8 Bring out the people who are blind, even though they have eyes, And the deaf, even though they have ears. (Isa 43:8 NAS)

- (i) The Word of God stands forever.
- (ii) Never losing its power and authority.

Section 2.09 Isaiah 55:11

(a) 11 So shall My word be which goes forth from My mouth; It shall not return to Me empty, without accomplishing what I desire, and without succeeding in the matter for which I sent it. (Isa 55:11 NAS)

- (i) The Word of God never comes back void.
- (ii) God always keeps His promises.

Section 2.10 J. Psalm 103:20

(a) 20 Bless the LORD, you His angels, Mighty in strength, who perform His word, Obeying the voice of His word! (Psa 103:20 NAS)
- (i) The Word is to be heeded.
- (ii) We should never take the Word of God for granted.

Section 2.11 K. 2 Peter 1:21

(a) 21 for no prophecy was ever made by an act of human will, but men moved by the Holy Spirit spoke from God. (2Pe 1:21 NAS)
- (i) 1. The Holy Spirit moved upon each writer in such a way that their words were indeed the very Word of God.

Section 2.12 L. Romans 15:4

(a) 4 For whatever was written in earlier times was written for our instruction, that through perseverance and the encouragement of the Scriptures we might have hope. (Rom 15:4 NAS
- (i))1. The Word of God is our rule of faith and conduct.

Article III. There is but One Living and True God
Section 3.01 A. Acts 17:24-25

(a) God that made the world and all things therein, seeing that he is Lord of heaven and earth, dwelleth not in temples made with hands; 25 Neither is worshipped with men's hands, as though he needed anything, seeing he giveth to all life, and breath, and all things; (Act 17:24-25 KJV)
- (i) This is his deity, the quality of having life in and from himself.
- (ii) God does not need any help from you and I.

Section 3.02 B. Psalm 18:24-25

(a) 24 Therefore hath the LORD recompensed me according to my righteousness, according to the cleanness of my hands in his eyesight. 25 With the merciful thou wilt shew thyself merciful; with an upright man thou wilt shew thyself upright; (Psa 18:24-25 KJV)

- (i) God is simple, perfect and immutable.
- (ii) His nature, goals, plans and ways of action do not change.

Section 3.03 C. John 3:16

(a) 16 For God so loved the world, that he gave his only begotten Son, that whosoever believeth in him should not perish, but have everlasting life. (Joh 3:16 KJV)

- (i) He is a God of Love.
- (ii) Holiness always qualifies this love.

Section 3.04 D. Hebrews 6:18

(a) 18 That by two immutable things, in which it was impossible for God to lie, we might have a strong consolation, who have fled for refuge to lay hold upon the hope set before us: (Heb 6:18 KJV)

- (i) 1. Because He is the true God, it I impossible for Him to lie.

Section 3.05 E. Numbers 24:16

(a) 16 He hath said, which heard the words of God, and knew the knowledge of the most High, which saw the vision of the Almighty, falling into a trance, but having his eyes open: (Num 24:16 KJV)

- (i) Elyon = The most High God
- (ii) There is only one person who is Most High and it is the Father Alone.

Section 3.06 A. Deuteronomy 6:4

(a) 4 Hear, O Israel: The LORD our God is one LORD: (Deu 6:4 KJV)

- (i) This aspect of oneness serves as the basis for prohibiting the worship of other gods or adding to the Father of All.
- (ii) This affirms that our Unbegotten God is the one and true God.

Section 3.07 C. Exodus 3:14

(a) *14 And God said unto Moses, I AM THAT I AM: and he said, Thus shalt thou say unto the children of Israel, I AM hath sent me unto you. (Exo 3:14 KJV)*

   (i) God is independent of all creation.
   (ii) This is expressing the unchanging, eternal self-existence of His being.
   (iii) God is not God because his substance is what qualifies him to be God. He is God because of who he is and no one else can be him.

Section 3.08 D. Deuteronomy 10:17

(a) *17 For the LORD your God is God of gods, and Lord of lords, a great God, a mighty, and a terrible, which regardeth not persons, nor taketh reward: (Deu 10:17 KJV)*

   (i) This shows us that the Unbegotten God is over all divine beings.
   (ii) God can not be bribed.

Section 3.09 E. Matthew 22:32

(a) *32 I am the God of Abraham, and the God of Isaac, and the God of Jacob? God is not the God of the dead, but of the living. (Mat 22:32 KJV)*

   (i) God is still living and active and not a God of lifeless things.
   (ii) Anything God is the God of is real and alive.
   (iii) God considers the patriarchs alive at this moment.

Section 3.10 F. Isaiah 12:2

(a) *2 Behold, God is my salvation; I will trust, and not be afraid: for the LORD JEHOVAH is my strength and my song; he also is become my salvation. (Isa 12:2 KJV)*

   (i) 1. Because He is the one living and true God, He is the God of our salvation.

Section 3.11 G. John 17:3

(a) And this is life eternal, that they might know thee the only true God, and Jesus Christ, whom thou hast sent. (Joh 17:3 KJV)

  (i) The Unbegotten Father is alone the True God.
  (ii) Jesus is not the True God.

Section 3.12 H. I Cor. 8:6

(a) 6 But to us there is but one God the Father, of whom are all things, and we in him; and one Lord Jesus Christ, by whom are all things, and we by him. (1Co 8:6 KJV)

  (i) There is only one true God in the bible and that is the Father alone.

Article IV. God Created All Things
Section 4.01 A. Revelation 4:11

(a) 11 Thou art worthy, O Lord, to receive glory and honour and power: for thou hast created all things, and for thy pleasure they are and were created. (Rev 4:11-1 KJV)

  (i) 1. Out of nothing God made the things that are, the universe, the elements,
  (ii) plant life, animal life and finally man in the image of God.

Section 4.02 B. Genesis 1:1

(a) In the beginning God created the heaven and the earth. (Gen 1:1 KJV)

  (i) The creation story teaches us much about God and us.
  (ii) First of all God is creative.
  (iii) God created all things within "the beginning creation" The Only begotten Divine Son Yeshua.
  (iv) This is how God the Father can say he "made all things alone" in Christ.

Section 4.03 C. Acts 17:25

- (a) 25 *Neither is worshipped with men's hands, as though he needed any thing, seeing he giveth to all life, and breath, and all things; (Act 17:25 KJV)*
  - (i) Creation was a free act of God; He did not need to do it.
  - (ii) He chose to do so not out of a need of anything but for his Son.

Section 4.04 D. Romans 9:5

- (a) *5 Whose are the fathers, and of whom as concerning the flesh Christ came, who is over all, God blessed for ever. Amen. (Rom 9:5 KJV)*
  - (i) 1. We must understand that although God has entrusted us to keep the Earth all things are still his.

Section 4.05 E. Acts 17:28

- (a) *28 For in him we live, and move, and have our being; as certain also of your own poets have said, For we are also his offspring. (Act 17:28 KJV)*
  - (i) 1. Even though He created everything He is also present within creation to sustain it.

Section 4.06 F. Psalm 33:6-9

- (a) *6 By the word of the LORD were the heavens made; and all the host of them by the breath of his mouth. 7 He gathereth the waters of the sea together as an heap: he layeth up the depth in storehouses. 8 Let all the earth fear the LORD: let all the inhabitants of the world stand in awe of him. 9 For he spake, and it was done; he commanded, and it stood fast. (Psa 33:6-9 KJV)*
  - (i) 1. God is not just the coordinator of natural forces; He is the Lord of creation, the Almighty God.

Section 4.07 A. Genesis 1:26

- (a) *26 And God said, Let us make man in our image, after our likeness: and let them have dominion over the fish of the sea, and over the fowl of the air, and over the cattle, and over all the earth, and over every creeping thing that creepeth upon the earth. (Gen 1:26 KJV)*

(i) When all was created it was the work done by the Father through the Son. God created in Christ all things and the Son brought forth each creation from himself.
(ii) The Bible says "let us" make man in our image not one God who is 3 persons. But The Only True God speaking to the True Son.

Section 4.08 B. Genesis 1:3-30

(a)   *.3 And God said, Let there be light: and there was light. 4 And God saw the light, that it was good: and God divided the light from the darkness. 5 And God called the light Day, and the darkness he called Night. And the evening and the morning were the first day. 6 And God said, Let there be a firmament in the midst of the waters, and let it divide the waters from the waters. 7 And God made the firmament, and divided the waters which were under the firmament from the waters which were above the firmament: and it was so. 8 And God called the firmament Heaven. And the evening and the morning were the second day. 9 And God said, Let the waters under the heaven be gathered together unto one place, and let the dry land appear: and it was so. 10 And God called the dry land Earth; and the gathering together of the waters called he Seas: and God saw that it was good. 11 And God said, Let the earth bring forth grass, the herb yielding seed, and the fruit tree yielding fruit after his kind, whose seed is in itself, upon the earth: and it was so. 12 And the earth brought forth grass, and herb yielding seed after his kind, and the tree yielding fruit, whose seed was in itself, after his kind: and God saw that it was good. 13 And the evening and the morning were the third day. 14 And God said, Let there be lights in the firmament of the heaven to divide the day from the night; and let them be for signs, and for seasons, and for days, and years: 15 And let them be for lights in the firmament of the heaven to give light upon the earth: and it was so. 16 And God made two great lights; the greater light to rule the day, and the lesser light to rule the night: he made the stars also. 17 And God set them in the firmament of the heaven to give light upon the earth, 18 And to rule over the day and over the night, and to divide the light from the darkness: and God saw that it was good. 19 And the evening and the morning were the fourth day. 20 And God said, Let the waters bring forth abundantly the moving creature that hath life, and fowl that may fly above the earth in the open firmament of heaven. 21 And God created great whales, and every living creature that moveth, which the waters brought forth abundantly, after their kind, and every winged fowl after his kind: and God saw that it was good. 22 And God blessed them, saying, Be fruitful, and multiply, and fill the waters in the seas, and let fowl multiply in the earth. 23 And the evening and the morning were the fifth day. 24 And God said, Let the earth bring forth the living creature after his kind, cattle, and*

(a) *creeping thing, and beast of the earth after his kind: and it was so. 25 And God made the beast of the earth after his kind, and cattle after their kind, and every thing that creepeth upon the earth after his kind: and God saw that it was good. 26 And God said, Let us make man in our image, after our likeness: and let them have dominion over the fish of the sea, and over the fowl of the air, and over the cattle, and over all the earth, and over every creeping thing that creepeth upon the earth. 27 So God created man in his own image, in the image of God created he him; male and female created he them. 28 And God blessed them, and God said unto them, Be fruitful, and multiply, and replenish the earth, and subdue it: and have dominion over the fish of the sea, and over the fowl of the air, and over every living thing that moveth upon the earth. 29 And God said, Behold, I have given you every herb bearing seed, which is upon the face of all the earth, and every tree, in the which is the fruit of a tree yielding seed; to you it shall be for meat. 30 And to every beast of the earth, and to every fowl of the air, and to every thing that creepeth upon the earth, wherein there is life, I have given every green herb for meat: and it was so. (Gen 1:3-30 KJV)*

- (i) These verses stress the orderliness and symmetry of God's creative activity.
- (ii) We serve a God of order today.

Section 4.09 C. Psalm 148:5

(a) *5 Let them praise the name of the LORD: for he commanded, and they were created. (Psa 148:5 KJV)*

- (i) All creation came into being at the express command of God to his Son.
- (ii) God has made their existence secure and established.

Section 4.10 D. Isaiah 7:14

(a) *14 Therefore the Lord himself shall give you a sign; Behold, a virgin shall conceive, and bear a son, and shall call his name Immanuel. (Isa 7:14 KJV)*

(i) 1. Because God is an eternal being He was able to transform his Son into another species and make him a descendant of David. A divine being with us.

Section 4.11 E. Hebrews 1:3

(a) 3 Who being the brightness of his glory, and the express image of his person, and upholding all things by the word of his power, when he had by himself purged our sins, sat down on the right hand of the Majesty on high; (Heb 1:3 KJV)

(i) 1. Not only did God create all things in heaven and on Earth, but created his Son after his own kind. To look identical to God but is a created being and not Unbegotten like the Father.

Section 4.12 F. Hebrews 11:3

(a) 3 Through faith we understand that the worlds were framed by the word of God, so that things which are seen were not made of things which do appear. (Heb 11:3 KJV)

(i) 1. There is no other kind of power over or against God or beyond His control.

Article V. In the divinity of the Lord Jesus Christ
Section 5.01 A. John 1:1-3

(a) 1 In the beginning was the Word, and the Word was with God, and the Word was God. 2 The same was in the beginning with God. 3 All things were made by him; and without him was not any thing made that was made. (Joh 1:1-3 KJV)

(i) The Lord Jesus Christ, the Son of God, was in divine form at the beginning before all things and has become fully human.
(ii) He is through whom all things were made.

Section 5.02 B. John 1:3

- (a) 3 *All things were made by him; and without him was not any thing made that was made. (Joh 1:3 KJV)*
    - (i) The visible universe with all its complexity owes its origin to the creative mind and power of God through his Son.
    - (ii) Apart from His Son nothing can exist nor has ever existed.

Section 5.03 C. Romans 9:5

- (a) 5 *Whose are the fathers, and of whom as concerning the flesh Christ came, who is over all, God blessed for ever. Amen. (Rom 9:5 KJV)*
    - (i) This indicates that culmination of all the promises given to us is seen in the person of Jesus Christ.
    - (ii) Each of these privileges finds its focus in Him.

Section 5.04 D. Titus 2:13

- (a) *while continuing to expect the blessed fulfillment of our certain hope, which is the appearing of the Sh'khinah of our great God and the appearing of our Deliverer, Yeshua the Messiah. (Tit 2:13 CJB)*
    - (i) God the Father will always get the glory, Christ glorifies the Unbegotten God.

Section 5.05 E. 1 John 5:1-20

(a) Whosoever believeth that Jesus is the Christ is born of God: and every one that loveth him that begat loveth him also that is begotten of him. 2 By this we know that we love the children of God, when we love God, and keep his commandments. 3 For this is the love of God, that we keep his commandments: and his commandments are not grievous. 4 For whatsoever is born of God overcometh the world: and this is the victory that overcometh the world, even our faith. 5 Who is he that overcometh the world, but he that believeth that Jesus is the Son of God? 6 This is he that came by water and blood, even Jesus Christ; not by water only, but by water and blood. And it is the Spirit that beareth witness, because the Spirit is truth. 7 For there are three that bear record ~~in heaven, the Father, the Word, and the Holy Ghost: and these three are one. 8 And there are three that bear witness in earth~~[1], the Spirit, and the water, and the blood: and these three agree in one. 9 If we receive the witness of men, the witness of God is greater: for this is the witness of God which he hath testified of his Son. 10 He that believeth on the Son of God hath the witness in himself: he that believeth not God hath made him a liar; because he believeth not the record that God gave of his Son. 11 And this is the record, that God hath given to us eternal life, and this life is in his Son. 12 He that hath the Son hath life; and he that hath not the Son of God hath not life. 13 These things have I written unto you that believe on the name of the Son of God; that ye may know that ye have eternal life, and that ye may believe on the name of the Son of God. 14 And this is the confidence that we have in him, that, if we ask any thing according to his will, he heareth us: 15 And if we know that he hear us, whatsoever we ask, we know that we have the petitions that we desired of him. 16 If any man see his brother sin a sin which is not unto death, he shall ask, and he shall give him life for them that sin not unto death. There is a sin unto death: I do not say that he shall pray for it. 17 All unrighteousness is sin: and there is a sin not unto death. 18 We know that whosoever is born of God sinneth not; but he that is begotten of God keepeth himself, and that wicked one toucheth him not. 19 And we know that we are of God, and the whole world lieth in wickedness. 20 And we know that the

---

[1] Trinitarian Corruption

Son of God is come, and hath given us an understanding, that we may know him that is true, and we are in him that is true, even in his Son Jesus Christ. This is the true God, and eternal life. (1Jo 5:1-20 KJV)

- (i) The purpose of all this assurance and certainty is so that we might enjoy knowledge of the true One the Father of all.
- (ii) He is infinitely superior in purity, power and perfection.

Section 5.06 F. Philippians 2:6

(a) *6 Who, being in the form of God, thought it not robbery to be equal with God: (Phi 2:6 KJV)*

- (i) 1. Even though Christ was equal with God in species and form but not uncreated but created, Christ left that divine form to become human.

Section 5.07 A. John 1:1

(a) *In the beginning was the Word, and the Word was with God, and the Word was God. (Joh 1:1 KJV)*

- (i) The Son is the Word, and he was at the beginning, but is not eternally always existed.
- (ii) Only the Father has always existed.

Section 5.08 John 1:18

(a) *18 No man has seen God at any time; the only born divinity who is in the lap of the Father, He has explained Him. (Joh 1:18)*

- (i) Jesus is a created divine being who is the true Son of God.

Section 5.09 C. Hebrews 1:3, Colossians 1:16

(a) *3 Who being the brightness of his glory, and the express image of his person, and upholding all things by the word of his power, when he had by himself purged our sins, sat down on the right hand of the Majesty on high; (Heb 1:3 KJV)*

(b) 16 *For by him were all things created, that are in heaven, and that are in earth, visible and invisible, whether they be thrones, or dominions, or principalities, or powers: all things were created by him, and for him: (Col 1:16 KJV)*

    (i) All things were intended to go to Christ.
    (ii) Jesus is not the Majesty on high but sits next to him.

Section 5.10 D. Hebrews 1:12, 13:8

(a) *12 And as a vesture shalt thou fold them up, and they shall be changed: but thou art the same, and thy years shall not fail. (Heb 1:12 KJV)*

(b) *8 Jesus Christ the same yesterday, and to day, and for ever. (Heb 13:8 KJV)*

    (i) Jesus is capable of committing sin but will never do so.
    (ii) Jesus will obey God.

Section 5.11 E. John 1:3

(a) *3 All things were made by him; and without him was not any thing made that was made. (Joh 1:3 KJV)*

    (i) We must respect Christ for his role in creation.

Section 5.12 F. Matthew 9:2-6

(a) *2 And, behold, they brought to him a man sick of the palsy, lying on a bed: and Jesus seeing their faith said unto the sick of the palsy; Son, be of good cheer; thy sins be forgiven thee. 3 And, behold, certain of the scribes said within themselves, This man blasphemeth. 4 And Jesus knowing their thoughts said, Wherefore think ye evil in your hearts? 5 For whether is easier, to say, Thy sins be forgiven thee; or to say, Arise, and walk? 6 But that ye may know that the Son of man hath power on earth to forgive sins, (then saith he to the sick of the palsy,) Arise, take up thy bed, and go unto thine house. (Mat 9:2-6 KJV)*

    (i) Jesus can forgives sins.

Section 5.13 G. John 17:3

(a) *3 And this is life eternal, that they might know thee the only true God, and Jesus Christ, whom thou hast sent. (Joh 17:3 KJV)*

    (i) Jesus teaches that the Father of All is the Only True GOD excluding himself.

Section 5.14 H. Luke 18:19

(a) *19 And Jesus said unto him, Why callest thou me good? none is good, save one, that is, God. (Luk 18:19 KJV)*

    (i) Jesus is saying he is not consubstantial with God. And he cannot receive the praise due the true God.

Section 5.15 I. John 20:17

(a) *17 Jesus saith unto her, Touch me not; for I am not yet ascended to my Father: but go to my brethren, and say unto them, I ascend unto my Father, and your Father; and to my God, and your God. (Joh 20:17 KJV)*

    (i) Jesus is saying that we have the same Father and we have the same God. That the same way we all share a Father we all share the same one God.

Section 5.16 A. Matthew 1:23

(a) *23 Behold, a virgin shall be with child, and shall bring forth a son, and they shall call his name Emmanuel, which being interpreted is, God with us. (Mat 1:23 KJV)*

    (i) He was born of a virgin.
    (ii) The virgin birth of Christ is undoubtedly the most essential doctrine underling his Divinity. "Divinity with us"

Section 5.17 B. II Corinthians 5:21

(a) *21 For he hath made him to be sin for us, who knew no sin; that we might be made the righteousness of God in him. (2Co 5:21 KJV)*

    (i) He led a sinless life.

(ii) This imputation helps us understand Christ's struggle in the Garden of Gethsemane with the death payment for the wages of our sin which would be upon Him on the cross.

Section 5.18 C. John 11:47

(a) *47 Then gathered the chief priests and the Pharisees a council, and said, What do we? for this man doeth many miracles. (Joh 11:47 KJV)*

(i) He performed miracles.
(ii) He is still performing miracles today.

Section 5.19 D. Matthew 26:28

(a) *28 For this is my blood of the new testament, which is shed for many for the remission of sins. (Mat 26:28 KJV)*

(i) He died on the cross for our sins.
(ii) We have been set free from sin. (Romans 8:9-11)

Section 5.20 E. Matthew 28:6

(a) *6 He is not here: for he is risen, as he said. Come, see the place where the Lord lay. (Mat 28:6 KJV)*

(i) He rose bodily from the dead.
(ii) We serve a living Lord today.

Section 5.21 F. Acts 2:37

(a) *37 Now when they heard this, they were pricked in their heart, and said unto Peter and to the rest of the apostles, Men and brethren, what shall we do? (Act 2:37 KJV)*

(i) He sits at the right hand of the Father and the Holy Spirit convicts the world of its sin.

Article VI. In the Sinfulness of Man
Section 6.01 A. I John 3:9

(a) 9 *Whosoever is born of God doth not commit sin; for his seed remaineth in him: and he cannot sin, because he is born of God. (1Jo 3:9 KJV)*

- (i) In spite of our sinful nature, we can look forward to victory over sin.
- (ii) The secret is that we must stay in harmony with the word of God.

Section 6.02 B. II Corinthians 5:17

(a) *17 Therefore if any man be in Christ, he is a new creature: old things are passed away; behold, all things are become new. (2Co 5:17 KJV)*

- (i) Righteousness cannot mix with darkness.
- (ii) The old nature has to die.

Section 6.03 C. Romans 12:2

(a) *2 And be not conformed to this world: but be ye transformed by the renewing of your mind, that ye may prove what is that good, and acceptable, and perfect, will of God. (Rom 12:2 KJV)*

- (i) 1. Unless we allow the Word of God to change us the old nature will do everything possible to come up.

Section 6.04 D. Jeremiah 17:9

(a) *9 The heart is deceitful above all things, and desperately wicked: who can know it? (Jer 17:9 KJV)*

- (i) **1. A sinful nature is attributed to a deceitful and wicked heart**.

Section 6.05 E. Proverbs 10:24

(a) *24 The fear of the wicked, it shall come upon him: but the desire of the righteous shall be granted. (Pro 10:24 KJV)*

- (i) You can rest assured that the sinful nature will come back to haunt you if you allow it to.
- (ii) We should all desire that the old man never over power us.

Section 6.06 A. Genesis 3:6

- (a) 6 And when the woman saw that the tree was good for food, and that it was pleasant to the eyes, and a tree to be desired to make one wise, she took of the fruit thereof, and did eat, and gave also unto her husband with her; and he did eat. (Gen 3:6 KJV)
  - (i) 1. Adam unlike Eve was not deceived but sinned deliberately.

Section 6.07 B. Jeremiah 17:9

- (a) 9 The heart is deceitful above all things, and desperately wicked: who can know it? (Jer 17:9 KJV)
  - (i) 1. Sin is like a cancer, in that it will eat you up alive.

Section 6.08 C. Romans 8:7

- (a) 7 Because the carnal mind is enmity against God: for it is not subject to the law of God, neither indeed can be. (Rom 8:7 KJV)
  - (i) All sin directed against God.
  - (ii) There are always consequences for our sins.

Section 6.09 D. Proverbs 3:5

- (a) 5 Trust in the LORD with all thine heart; and lean not unto thine own understanding. (Pro 3:5 KJV)
  - (i) 1. Because of the sinful nature that abides in us we too are bent on doing things our own way.

Section 6.10 E. Romans 8:3

- (a) 3 For what the law could not do, in that it was weak through the flesh, God sending his own Son in the likeness of sinful flesh, and for sin, condemned sin in the flesh: (Rom 8:3 KJV)
  - (i) Our goal is to not walk in the flesh but in the Spirit.
  - (ii) The Lord did what the law could not do.

Section 6.11 F. I John 1:8

- (a) 8 If we say that we have no sin, we deceive ourselves, and the truth is not in us. (1Jo 1:8 KJV)

- (i) In order for God to cleanse us of sin, we must first acknowledge it.
- (ii) We can not live in denial.

Section 6.12 G. Acts 17:30

(a) 30 And the times of this ignorance God winked at; but now commandeth all men every where to repent: (Act 17:30 KJV)

- (i) 1. We need to repent daily.

Article VII.   In the Salvation of Man
Section 7.01 A. John 3:16

(a) 16 For God so loved the world, that he gave his only begotten Son, that whosoever believeth in him should not perish, but have everlasting life. (Joh 3:16 KJV)

- (i) This is the heart of the Gospel.
- (ii) The source of Love – God
- (iii) The extent of Love – The world
- (iv) The sacrifice of Love – He gave His only begotten Son.
- (v) The results of Love – Whosoever believeth in Him shall not perish.

Section 7.02 B. Matthew 3:2

(a) 2 And saying, Repent ye: for the kingdom of heaven is at hand. (Mat 3:2 KJV)

- (i) Salvation comes through repentance.
- (ii) We must be careful not to confuse repentance with regret.
- (iii) Repent = turn away from sin
- (iv) Regret = Sorry you were caught.

Section 7.03 C. Luke 8:12

(a) 12 Those by the way side are they that hear; then cometh the devil, and taketh away the word out of their hearts, lest they should believe and be saved. (Luk 8:12 KJV)

(i) 1. Salvation is found in the person and work of Jesus Christ.
(ii) His life,
(iii) His Ministry
(iv) His vicarious death
(v) His resurrection.

Section 7.04 D. Romans 10:9-10

(a) 9 That if thou shalt confess with thy mouth the Lord Jesus, and shalt believe in thine heart that God hath raised him from the dead, thou shalt be saved. 10 For with the heart man believeth unto righteousness; and with the mouth confession is made unto salvation. (Rom 10:9-10 KJV)

(i) Those who call on the Lord will be saved.
(ii) Confession with the mouth is evidence of genuine faith in the heart.

Section 7.05 E. Titus 3:5

(a) 5 Not by works of righteousness which we have done, but according to his mercy he saved us, by the washing of regeneration, and renewing of the Holy Ghost; (Tit 3:5 KJV)

(i) Salvation is dependent on the Grace of God.
(ii) We cannot save ourselves by our own efforts.

Section 7.06 A. Philippians 2:12

(a) 12 Wherefore, my beloved, as ye have always obeyed, not as in my presence only, but now much more in my absence, work out your own salvation with fear and trembling. (Phi 2:12 KJV)

(i) We can not view salvations as once saved always saved.
(ii) This misconception misleads many people in our churches today.

Section 7.07 B. Here are five conditions of eternal salvation.

1. Luke 8:12

(a) *12 Those by the way side are they that hear; then cometh the devil, and taketh away the word out of their hearts, lest they should believe and be saved. (Luk 8:12 KJV)*

    (i) Hear the word of God.
    (ii) Be honest with yourself.

2. Romans 6:16-23

(b) *16 Know ye not, that to whom ye yield yourselves servants to obey, his servants ye are to whom ye obey; whether of sin unto death, or of obedience unto righteousness? 17 But God be thanked, that ye were the servants of sin, but ye have obeyed from the heart that form of doctrine which was delivered you. 18 Being then made free from sin, ye became the servants of righteousness. 19 I speak after the manner of men because of the infirmity of your flesh: for as ye have yielded your members servants to uncleanness and to iniquity unto iniquity; even so now yield your members servants to righteousness unto holiness. 20 For when ye were the servants of sin, ye were free from righteousness. 21 What fruit had ye then in those things whereof ye are now ashamed? for the end of those things is death. 22 But now being made free from sin, and become servants to God, ye have your fruit unto holiness, and the end everlasting life. 23 For the wages of sin is death; but the gift of God is eternal life through Jesus Christ our Lord. (Rom 6:16-23 KJV)*

    (i) Maintain an honest and good heart.
    (ii) This can be hard because our hearts are wicked and deceitful.

3. John 15:7

(c) *7 If ye abide in me, and my words abide in you, ye shall ask what ye will, and it shall be done unto you. (Joh 15:7 KJV)*

    (i) Keep the Word of God in our hearts.
    (ii) This is why we need to meditate on the Word of God and study it.

4. Hebrews 3:6

(d) *6 But Christ as a son over his own house; whose house are we, if we hold fast the confidence and the rejoicing of the hope firm unto the end. (Heb 3:6 KJV)*

    (i) We must be rooted and grounded in the Truth.
    (ii) If we know our doctrine, we are less likely to be persuaded by another.

5. Romans 1:16

- (e) 16 For I am not ashamed of the gospel of Christ: for it is the power of God unto salvation to every one that believeth; to the Jew first, and also to the Greek. (Rom 1:16 KJV)
  - (i) a. Obey the Word of God.

Article VIII. In the Sanctification of the Believer
Section 8.01 A. Ephesians 1:4

- (a) 4 According as he hath chosen us in him before the foundation of the world, that we should be holy and without blame before him in love: (Eph 1:4 KJV)
  - (i) Paul traces mans salvation back to the plan of God's will.
  - (ii) Sanctification and salvation – we can't have one without the other.

Section 8.02 B. I Corinthians 1:30

- (a) 30 But of him are ye in Christ Jesus, who of God is made unto us wisdom, and righteousness, and sanctification, and redemption: (1Co 1:30 KJV)
  - (i) Sanctification contemplates the work of Christ in the believer.
  - (ii) Sanctification is an on going process.

Section 8.03 C. Galatians 5:11

- (a) 13 For you were called to freedom, brethren; only do not turn your freedom into an opportunity for the flesh, but through love serve one another. 14 For the whole Law is fulfilled in one word, in the statement, "You shall love your neighbor as yourself." 15 But if you bite and devour one another, take care lest you be consumed by one another. 16 But I say, walk by the Spirit, and you will not carry out the desire of the flesh. 17 For the flesh sets its desire against the Spirit, and the Spirit against the flesh; for these are in opposition to one another, so that you may not do the things that you please. 18 But if you are led by the Spirit, you are not under the Law. (Gal 5:13-18 NAS)

(i) 1. Sanctification is progressive in the life of the believer. (This means that it is gradually increasing.)

Section 8.04 D. I Thessalonians 4:3

(a) *3 For this is the will of God, even your sanctification, that ye should abstain from fornication: (1Th 4:3 KJV)*

(i) All believers have been called to be sanctified.
(ii) This is God's will.

Section 8.05 E. John 10:36

(a) *36 Say ye of him, whom the Father hath sanctified, and sent into the world, Thou blasphemest; because I said, I am the Son of God? (Joh 10:36 KJV)*

(i) The Father set Christ apart for the work of salvation, Christ has never had sin.

Section 8.06 F. John 17:19

(a) *19 And for their sakes I sanctify myself, that they also might be sanctified through the truth. (Joh 17:19 KJV)*

(i) 1. Sanctification of the believer is seen primarily as the work of Christ.

Section 8.07 G. Romans 15:16

(a) *16 That I should be the minister of Jesus Christ to the Gentiles, ministering the gospel of God, that the offering up of the Gentiles might be acceptable, being sanctified by the Holy Ghost. (Rom 15:16 KJV)*

(i) 1. Sanctification of the believer is seen primarily as the work of the Holy Spirit.

Section 8.08 A. I Corinthians 1:30

(a) *30 But of him are ye in Christ Jesus, who of God is made unto us wisdom, and righteousness, and sanctification, and redemption: (1Co 1:30 KJV)*

(i) When we receive Christ.

(ii) But we must allow Him to become the Lord of our lives.

Section 8.09 B. Romans 6:3

(a) 3 *Know ye not, that so many of us as were baptized into Jesus Christ were baptized into his death? (Rom 6:3 KJV)*

(i) 1. When we are baptized we have buried our old sinful life and now live after the Spirit who is helping us live holy lives.

Section 8.10 C. Acts 26:18

(a) 18 *To open their eyes, and to turn them from darkness to light, and from the power of Satan unto God, that they may receive forgiveness of sins, and inheritance among them which are sanctified by faith that is in me. (Act 26:18 KJV)*

(i) 1. When we turn from Satan to God at the forgiveness of sins we begin the life in the light. (Remember repentance is the key here.)

Section 8.11 D. Hebrews 10:29

(a) 29 *Of how much sorer punishment, suppose ye, shall he be thought worthy, who hath trodden under foot the Son of God, and hath counted the blood of the covenant, wherewith he was sanctified, an unholy thing, and hath done despite unto the Spirit of grace? (Heb 10:29 KJV)*

(i) When we are cleansed by the blood of Jesus we must not disgrace the Son of God by continuing a life of sin.
(ii) There is power in blood of Jesus and great anger if we take the blood for granted.

Section 8.12 E. I Corinthians 3:16-17

(a) 16 *Know ye not that ye are the temple of God, and that the Spirit of God dwelleth in you? 17 If any man defile the temple of God, him shall God destroy; for the temple of God is holy, which temple ye are. (1Co 3:16-17 KJV)*

(i) When are temples of God, we must keep the Temple honourable.

(ii) We are to remain sanctified unto the Lord.

Section 8.13 F. Titus 2:11-12

(a) 11 For the grace of God that bringeth salvation hath appeared to all men, 12 Teaching us that, denying ungodliness and worldly lusts, we should live soberly, righteously, and godly, in this present world; (Tit 2:11-12 KJV)

- (i) When grace brings salvation and the Spirit renews us.
- (ii) Even though we are in the world, we are no longer of the world and our desires are not set on its systems or its values.

Article IX. In the Baptism of the Holy Spirit
Section 9.01 A. John 7:37-39

(a) 37 In the last day, that great day of the feast, Jesus stood and cried, saying, If any man thirst, let him come unto me, and drink. 38 He that believeth on me, as the scripture hath said, out of his belly shall flow rivers of living water. 39 (But this spake he of the Spirit, which they that believe on him should receive: for the Holy Ghost was not yet given; because that Jesus was not yet glorified.) (Joh 7:37-39 KJV)

- (i) Jesus promised this to all who would believe in Him.
- (ii) It comes by faith.

Section 9.02 B. Acts 1:12

(a) 12 Then returned they unto Jerusalem from the mount called Olivet, which is from Jerusalem a sabbath day's journey. (Act 1:12 KJV)

- (i) Jesus had to be crucified so that we could receive this Baptism.
- (ii) This is one of the blessings we are given because of His death and resurrection.

Section 9.03 C. Galatians 3:14

(a) 14 *That the blessing of Abraham might come on the Gentiles through Jesus Christ; that we might receive the promise of the Spirit through faith. (Gal 3:14 KJV)*

   (i) 1. Faith is the key factor here.

Section 9.04 D. Acts 1:18

(a) 18 *Now this man purchased a field with the reward of iniquity; and falling headlong, he burst asunder in the midst, and all his bowels gushed out. (Act 1:18 KJV)*

   (i) Judas lacked sanctification and the Spirit he is an example of unholy living in the presence of God and Christ.

Section 9.05 E. John 7:37,38

(a) 37 *In the last day, that great day of the feast, Jesus stood and cried, saying, If any man thirst, let him come unto me, and drink. 38 He that believeth on me, as the scripture hath said, out of his belly shall flow rivers of living water. (Joh 7:37-38 KJV)*

   (i) 1. Here are four conditions for receiving the baptism of the Holy Spirit.
   (ii) (v.37) Thirst = we need to have the burning passion within ourselves.
   (iii) (v.37) Come unto Me = this means a complete surrender of ourselves, to do the will of God.
   (iv) (v.37) Drinks = this means the wholehearted reception into ones life of the gifts, the fruits, and operations of the Holy Spirit.
   (v) (v.38) Believes in me and the Scriptures = to believe in the whole Gospel.

Section 9.06 A. Acts 2:38,39

(a) 38 *Then Peter said unto them, Repent, and be baptized every one of you in the name of Jesus Christ for the remission of sins, and ye shall receive the gift of the Holy Ghost.*

(b) 39 *For the promise is unto you, and to your children, and to all that are afar off, even as many as the Lord our God shall call. (Act 2:38-39 KJV)*

   (i) We have got to have faith that this promise is for us.

(ii) A persistency of faith that will not be denied.

Section 9.07 B. Acts 2:1-4

(a) 1 And when the day of Pentecost was fully come, they were all with one accord in one place. 2 And suddenly there came a sound from heaven as of a rushing mighty wind, and it filled all the house where they were sitting. 3 And there appeared unto them cloven tongues like as of fire, and it sat upon each of them. 4 And they were all filled with the Holy Ghost, and began to speak with other tongues, as the Spirit gave them utterance. (Act 2:1-4 KJV)

(i) The key here is that we have got to expect it, to get it.
(ii) The Baptism may come suddenly, while sitting and not expecting Him to come.

Section 9.08 C. Acts 10:14-17

(a) 14 But Peter said, Not so, Lord; for I have never eaten any thing that is common or unclean. 15 And the voice spake unto him again the second time, What God hath cleansed, that call not thou common. 16 This was done thrice: and the vessel was received up again into heaven. 17 Now while Peter doubted in himself what this vision which he had seen should mean, behold, the men which were sent from Cornelius had made enquiry for Simon's house, and stood before the gate, (Act 10:14-17 KJV)

(i) It can come through prayer and lying on of the hands.
(ii) It can come when an alter call is made.

Section 9.09 D. Acts 10:44-46

(a) 44 While Peter yet spake these words, the Holy Ghost fell on all them which heard the word. 45 And they of the circumcision which believed were astonished, as many as came with Peter, because that on the Gentiles also was poured out the gift of the Holy Ghost. 46 For they heard them speak with tongues, and magnify God. Then answered Peter, (Act 10:44-46 KJV)

(i) It can come instantly and unexpectedly while listening to a sermon.
(ii) Your heart has to be open.

Section 9.10 E. Acts 2:4

(a) 4 And they were all filled with the Holy Ghost, and began to speak with other tongues, as the Spirit gave them utterance. (Act 2:4 KJV)

- (i) 1. An evidence and result of the baptism with the Holy Spirit, is speaking with other tongues as the Spirit gives utterance.
- (ii) But it does not happen to everyone.
- (iii) And it is not a requirement it is by faith.

Section 9.11 F. Acts 2:11

(a) 11 Cretes and Arabians, we do hear them speak in our tongues the wonderful works of God. (Act 2:11 KJV)

- (i) This evidence will include praises to God.
- (ii) This can also be accompanied by an over flowing joy of the Lord.

Article X.   In the Church and its Mission
Section 10.01   A. Matthew 16:18

(a) 18 And I say also unto thee, That thou art Peter, and upon this rock I will build my church; and the gates of hell shall not prevail against it. (Mat 16:18 KJV)

- (i) 1. The church is a people called to lay the truth at the foundation that Jesus is the Son of God nothing about a trinity here. If you lay as your foundation a Son who is God Almighty your building on sifting sand.

Section 10.02   B. II Corinthians 6:16-18

(a) 16 And what agreement hath the temple of God with idols? for ye are the temple of the living God; as God hath said, I will dwell in them, and walk in them; and I will be their God, and they shall be my people. 17 Wherefore come out from among them, and be ye separate, saith the Lord, and touch not the unclean thing; and I will receive you, 18 And will be a Father unto you, and ye shall be my sons and daughters, saith the Lord Almighty. (2Co 6:16-1 KJV)

- (i) The Condition – if we do not touch the unclean things.
- (ii) The Promise – I will receive you.

Section 10.03   C. I Corinthians 6:15-16

(a) 15 Know ye not that your bodies are the members of Christ? shall I then take the members of Christ, and make them the members of an harlot? God forbid. 16 What? know ye not that he which is joined to an harlot is one body? for two, saith he, shall be one flesh. (1Co 6:15-16 KJV)

- (i) We are the body of Christ. Jesus is not commiting adultery nor fornication and we shouldnt either with Christs body.

Section 10.04   D. I Corinthians 3:16

(a) 16 Know ye not that ye are the temple of God, and that the Spirit of God dwelleth in you? (1Co 3:16 KJV)

- (i) 1. In the midst of this corrupt society, we have a purpose, that is to reach out to those in darkness in the power of the Holy Spirit.

Section 10.05   E. Mark 16:15

(a) 15 And he said unto them, Go ye into all the world, and preach the gospel to every creature. (Mar 16:15 KJV)

- (i) One of our core values is evangelism
- **(ii)** That is what Jesus said we should do. **(Matthew 23:18)**

Section 10.06   F. Acts 5:42

(a) 42 And daily in the temple, and in every house, they ceased not to teach and preach Jesus Christ. (Act 5:42 KJV)

- (i) The primary mission of the church is to preach the Gospel.
- (ii) The same message of hope that touched you and me.

Section 10.07   A. Acts 11:22

(a) 22 *Then tidings of these things came unto the ears of the church which was in Jerusalem: and they sent forth Barnabas, that he should go as far as Antioch. (Act 11:22 KJV)*

- (i) This is the mother church of Christianity
- (ii) We are not to do anything different than what they did.

Section 10.08   B. II Corinthians 11:2

(a) *2 For I am jealous over you with godly jealousy: for I have espoused you to one husband, that I may present you as a chaste virgin to Christ. (2Co 11:2 KJV)*

- (i) This marriage image emphasizes the devotion and faithfulness of the church to Christ.
- (ii) Describes Christ's love with the church.

Section 10.09   C. John 14:12-14

(a) *12 Verily, verily, I say unto you, He that believeth on me, the works that I do shall he do also; and greater works than these shall he do; because I go unto my Father. 13 And whatsoever ye shall ask in my name, that will I do, that the Father may be glorified in the Son. 14 If ye shall ask any thing in my name, I will do it. (Joh 14:12-14 KJV)*

- (i) The signs and wonders that Christ displayed God can also do through us today as a witness to our testimony.
- (ii) We must have confidence in the Faithfulness of Christ on our behalf to assist us to the glory of God the Father.

Section 10.10   D. Hebrews 13:12-14

(a) *12 Wherefore Jesus also, that he might sanctify the people with his own blood, suffered without the gate. 13 Let us go forth therefore unto him without the camp, bearing his reproach. 14 For here have we no continuing city, but we seek one to come. (Heb 13:12-14 KJV)*

- (i) 1. The camp is symbolic of two things.
- (ii) The world with all of its sinful pleasures, ungodly values and temporal goals we live outside this camp.
- (iii) In going outside the gate, we find ourselves strangers and aliens to the world.

Section 10.11   E. Acts 1:8

(a) *8 But ye shall receive power, after that the Holy Ghost is come upon you: and ye shall be witnesses unto me both in Jerusalem, and in all Judaea, and in Samaria, and unto the uttermost part of the earth. (Act 1:8 KJV)*

  (i) The church, are those regenerated people, who are gathered together in Christ.
  (ii) This is where the Gospel is preached and believers are nurtured by the power of the Holy Spirit.

Section 10.12   A. Matthew 28:19

(a) *19 Go ye therefore, and teach all nations, baptizing them in the name of the Father, and of the Son, and of the Holy Ghost: (Mat 28:19 KJV)*

  (i) Water baptism by immersion.
  (ii) This was part of the great commission to the disciples.

Section 10.13   B. Romans 6:1-5

(a) *What shall we say then? Shall we continue in sin, that grace may abound? 2 God forbid. How shall we, that are dead to sin, live any longer therein? 3 Know ye not, that so many of us as were baptized into Jesus Christ were baptized into his death? 4 Therefore we are buried with him by baptism into death: that like as Christ was raised up from the dead by the glory of the Father, even so we also should walk in newness of life. 5 For if we have been planted together in the likeness of his death, we shall be also in the likeness of his resurrection: (Rom 6:1-5 KJV)*

  (i) The symbolism of the baptism.
  (ii) Baptism is a picture of a burial and a resurrection.
  (iii) It is a picture of a birth.

Section 10.14   C. Acts 2:38

(a) 38 *Then Peter said unto them, Repent, and be baptized every one of you in the name of Jesus Christ for the remission of sins, and ye shall receive the gift of the Holy Ghost. (Act 2:38 KJV)*

    (i) The person being baptized should be a penitent believer.
    (ii) He must have repented of all his sins.

Section 10.15   D. Mark 16:16

(a) *16 He that believeth and is baptized shall be saved; but he that believeth not shall be damned. (Mar 16:16 KJV)*

    (i) This is the proper purpose of baptism.
    (ii) For symbolically accepting judgment of sins for the unbeliever.

Section 10.16   E. Romans 3:24

(a) *24 Being justified freely by his grace through the redemption that is in Christ Jesus: (Rom 3:24 KJV)*

    (i) 1. The Bible says that redemption is in Christ, and not to be found elsewhere.

Section 10.17   F. II Corinthians 5:17

(a) *17 Therefore if any man be in Christ, he is a new creature: old things are passed away; behold, all things are become new. (2Co 5:17 KJV)*

    (i) 1. We are all created anew.

Article XI.   In the Ordinances of the Church

Section 11.01   A. I Corinthians 11:24

(a) *24 And when he had given thanks, he brake it, and said, Take, eat: this is my body, which is broken for you: this do in remembrance of me. (1Co 11:24 KJV)*

    (i) The Lords' Supper is a memorial supper, recalling and portraying Christ's death for sinners.
    (ii) A memorial is something that keeps alive the memory of a person or an event.

Section 11.02   B. I Corinthians 5:6-8

(a) *6 Your glorying is not good. Know ye not that a little leaven leaveneth the whole lump? 7 Purge out therefore the old leaven, that ye may be a new lump, as ye are unleavened. For even Christ our passover is sacrificed for us: 8 Therefore let us keep the feast, not with old leaven, neither with the leaven of malice and wickedness; but with the unleavened bread of sincerity and truth. (1Co 5:6-8 KJV)*

   (i) 1. The Bread = unleavened bread this was to remind them of their hasty departure from Egypt. And the call to be holy and without hierocracy.
   (ii) The body we accept from Christ is symbolic of our new body that we share with Christ at the resurrection. As Eve shared flesh of Adam we will share flesh with the Last Adam in eternity.

Section 11.03   C. Mark 14:23-25

(a) *23 And he took the cup, and when he had given thanks, he gave it to them: and they all drank of it. 24 And he said unto them, This is my blood of the new testament, which is shed for many. 25 Verily I say unto you, I will drink no more of the fruit of the vine, until that day that I drink it new in the kingdom of God. (Mar 14:23-25 KJV)*

   (i) The fruit of the vine.
   (ii) It is significant that Jesus chose the blood of the grape to picture the "Blood of the Covenant" as our Saviors blood.
   (iii) The symbolic acceptance of his atoning blood.

Section 11.04   D. I Corinthians 10:16

(a) *16 The cup of blessing which we bless, is it not the communion of the blood of Christ? The bread which we break, is it not the communion of the body of Christ? (1Co 10:16 KJV)*

   (i) The breaking of the bread.
   (ii) The following day when the body of Jesus was cut and pierced, the Apostles had a graphic picture of what Jesus meant.

Section 11.05   E. I Corinthians 15:3

(a) 3 *For I delivered unto you first of all that which I also received, how that Christ died for our sins according to the scriptures; (1Co 15:3 KJV)*

    (i) 1. By the symbolic impact it constantly reminds us of the significant fact of Christianity.

Section 11.06   F. I Corinthians 11:24

(a) *24 And when he had given thanks, he brake it, and said, Take, eat: this is my body, which is broken for you: this do in remembrance of me. (1Co 11:24 KJV)*

    (i) 1. It satisfies the desires of the heart to do something honoring of our Saviors suffering for us.

Article XII.   In Divine Healing:

(a) *Healing means the restoration of an ill person to full health in body or mind or both.*

Section 12.02   A. Romans 12:2

(a) *2 And be not conformed to this world: but be ye transformed by the renewing of your mind, that ye may prove what is that good, and acceptable, and perfect, will of God. (Rom 12:2 KJV)*

    (i) The Word of God is what cleanses our minds.
    (ii) When the Word of God is removing ungodly thoughts, it is putting in Godly thoughts.

Section 12.03   B. Psalm 119:105

(a) *105 NUN. Thy word is a lamp unto my feet, and a light unto my path. (Psa 119:105 KJV)*

    (i) 1. The Word of God will continue to guild us in His marvelous light.

Section 12.04   C. Ephesians 6:17

(a) *17 And take the helmet of salvation, and the sword of the Spirit, which is the word of God: (Eph 6:17 KJV)*

(i) The Word of God is a powerful offensive weapon that God has given us to fight off the devil.

(ii) It is important that we know the Word of God and how to use it.

Section 12.05   D. Hebrews 4:12

(a) *12 For the word of God is quick, and powerful, and sharper than any twoedged sword, piercing even to the dividing asunder of soul and spirit, and of the joints and marrow, and is a discerner of the thoughts and intents of the heart. (Heb 4:12 KJV)*

(i) The Word of God exposes us.

(ii) There is no part of man that the Word of God cannot penetrate.

Section 12.06   E. James 1:22

(a) *22 But be ye doers of the word, and not hearers only, deceiving your own selves. (Jam 1:22 KJV)*

(i) Being hearers is not enough; we must also be doers of the word.

(ii) We must apply the Word of God to our lives daily.

Section 12.07   F. Matthew 7:25

(a) *25 And the rain descended, and the floods came, and the winds blew, and beat upon that house; and it fell not: for it was founded upon a rock. (Mat 7:25 KJV)*

(i) We need to build our foundation upon the Word of God.

(ii) The Word of God will never let us down.

Section 12.08   A. Luke 18:43, Matthew 9:35

(a) *43 And immediately he received his sight, and followed him, glorifying God: and all the people, when they saw it, gave praise unto God. (Luk 18:43 KJV)*

(b) 35 *And Jesus went about all the cities and villages, teaching in their synagogues, and preaching the gospel of the kingdom, and healing every sickness and every disease among the people. (Mat 9:35 KJV)*

   (i) It takes the anointing of God to open the eyes of the blind.
   (ii) Healing can be instantaneous.
   (iii) Healing can be progressive. (Luke 17:14)

Section 12.09   B. James 5:15

(a) *15 And the prayer of faith shall save the sick, and the Lord shall raise him up; and if he have committed sins, they shall be forgiven him. (Jam 5:15 KJV)*

   (i) Healing and forgiveness go hand and hand.
   (ii) There is provision for physical healing as well as spiritual healing.

Section 12.10   C. Matthew 9:5

(a) *5 For whether is easier, to say, Thy sins be forgiven thee; or to say, Arise, and walk? (Mat 9:5 KJV)*

   (i) It is just as easy for God to heal the body as to save the soul.
   (ii) He wills to do both today on the same basis — Faith in the name of Jesus.

Section 12.11   D. Mark 5:23

(a) *23 And besought him greatly, saying, My little daughter lieth at the point of death: I pray thee, come and lay thy hands on her, that she may be healed; and she shall live. (Mar 5:23 KJV)*

   (i) Healing can come through the laying of hands.
   (ii) It was done back then and it can be done today.

Section 12.12   E. Matthew 5:28

27 after hearing about Jesus, came up in the crowd behind Him, and touched His cloak. 28 For she thought, "If I just touch His garments, I shall get well." 29 And immediately the flow of her blood was dried up; and she felt in her body that she was healed of her affliction. 30 And immediately Jesus, perceiving in Himself that the power proceeding from Him had gone forth, turned around in the crowd and said, "Who touched My garments?" 31 And His disciples said to Him, "You see the multitude pressing in on You, and You say, 'Who touched Me?'" 32 And He looked around to see the woman who had done this. 33 But the woman fearing and trembling, aware of what had happened to her, came and fell down before Him, and told Him the whole truth. 34 And He said to her, "Daughter, your faith has made you well; go in peace, and be healed of your affliction." (Mar 5:27-34 NAS)

- (i) The touch of faith is so different from the physical touch, but it is just as real.
- (ii) Someone can receive a healng through you and you not be aware someone is intending to be healed
- (iii) Jesus felt the healing virtue go out of Him.
- (iv) He knew that someone had touched him by faith.

Article XIII. In the Second Coming of Christ
Section 13.01   A. Matthew 24:27

(a) *27 For as the lightning cometh out of the east, and shineth even unto the west; so shall also the coming of the Son of man be.* (Mat 24:27 KJV)

- (i) The second coming deals with a physical return and not just a spiritual presence.
- (ii) This is when He comes to the Earth to judge the world.

Section 13.02   B. Matthew 24:36

(a) *36 But of that day and hour knoweth no man, no, not the angels of heaven, but my Father only.* (Mat 24:36 KJV)

(i) No one knows the time of His coming.
  (ii) Live each day as if he were coming that day.

Section 13.03   C. Revelation 1:7

(a) 7 Behold, he cometh with clouds; and every eye shall see him, and they also which pierced him: and all kindreds of the earth shall wail because of him. Even so, Amen. (Rev 1:7 KJV)

  (i) In the bodily manner He left, He will return in like manner.
  (ii) We are speaking of a literal return not a symbolic one.

Section 13.04   D. II Thessalonians 2:3

(a) 3 Let no man deceive you by any means: for that day shall not come, except there come a falling away first, and that man of sin be revealed, the son of perdition; (2Th 2:3 KJV)

  (i) 1. This speaks of the church losing many followers and the appearance of the antichrist.

Section 13.05   E. Revelation 13:5

(a) 5 And there was given unto him a mouth speaking great things and blasphemies; and power was given unto him to continue forty and two months. (Rev 13:5 KJV)

  (i) 1. There will be a false messiah inspired by Satan to perform miracles and blaspheme to claim divine honors he could be Jewish and a Priest in the Temple it could be anyone.

Section 13.06   F. II Thessalonians 2:8

(a) 8 And then shall that Wicked be revealed, whom the Lord shall consume with the spirit of his mouth, and shall destroy with the brightness of his coming (2Th 2:8 KJV)

  (i) 1. The second coming of Christ will see destruction of this figure and all evil.

Section 13.07   A. I Thessalonians 3:12,13

(a) 12 And the Lord make you to increase and abound in love one toward another, and toward all men, even as we do toward you: 13 To the end he may stablish your hearts unblameable in holiness before God, even our Father, at the coming of our Lord Jesus Christ with all his saints. (1Th 3:12-13 KJV)

  (i) For brotherly love.
  (ii) Our love should continue to grow beyond limits.

Section 13.08   B. Romans 13:12-14

(a) 12 The night is far spent, the day is at hand: let us therefore cast off the works of darkness, and let us put on the armour of light. 13 Let us walk honestly, as in the day; not in rioting and drunkenness, not in chambering and wantonness, not in strife and envying. 14 But put ye on the Lord Jesus Christ, and make not provision for the flesh, to fulfil the lusts thereof. (Rom 13:12-14 KJV)

  (i) Provokes holiness.
  (ii) Causes us to separate our lives unto the Lord and evangelize.

Section 13.09   C. Hebrews 10:25

(a) 25 Not forsaking the assembling of ourselves together, as the manner of some is; but exhorting one another: and so much the more, as ye see the day approaching. (Heb 10:25 KJV)

  (i) Encourage meeting together.
  (ii) The assembling of the believers is often an outward indication of the inner condition.
    1) (IF A MAN'S FAITH WILL NOT GET HIM TO CHURCH IT IS DOUBTFUL IF IT WILL GET HIM TO HEAVEN.)

Section 13.10   D. II Timothy 4:1-2

(a) *I charge thee therefore before God, and the Lord Jesus Christ, who shall judge the quick and the dead at his appearing and his kingdom; 2 Preach the word; be instant in season, out of season; reprove, rebuke, exhort with all longsuffering and doctrine. (2Ti 4:1-2 KJV)*

   (i) 1. Faithfulness in ministry.

Section 13.11   E. I Thessalonians 4:14-18

(a) *14 For if we believe that Jesus died and rose again, even so them also which sleep in Jesus will God bring with him. 15 For this we say unto you by the word of the Lord, that we which are alive and remain unto the coming of the Lord shall not prevent them which are asleep. 16 For the Lord himself shall descend from heaven with a shout, with the voice of the archangel, and with the trump of God: and the dead in Christ shall rise first: 17 Then we which are alive and remain shall be caught up together with them in the clouds, to meet the Lord in the air: and so shall we ever be with the Lord. 18 Wherefore comfort one another with these words. (1Th 4:14-18 KJV)*

   (i) Comfort for the bereaved.
   (ii) The dead will also resurrect as Jesus did.

Section 13.12   A. Revelation 1:7

(a) *7 Behold, he cometh with clouds; and every eye shall see him, and they also which pierced him: and all kindreds of the earth shall wail because of him. Even so, Amen. (Rev 1:7 KJV)*

   (i) His coming will be personal, visible and glorious.
   (ii) We should all be looking forward to this.
      1) THIS IS NOT ONLY FOR THE LIVING BUT FOR THE DEAD ALSO.

Section 13.13   B. I Thessalonians 4:16-18

(a) 16 *For the Lord himself shall descend from heaven with a shout, with the voice of the archangel, and with the trump of God: and the dead in Christ shall rise first: 17 Then we which are alive and remain shall be caught up together with them in the clouds, to meet the Lord in the air: and so shall we ever be with the Lord. 18 Wherefore comfort one another with these words* (1Th 4:16-18 KJV)

- (i) The dead in Christ will rise, then the redeemed that are alive shall be caught up together to meet the Lord in the air.
- (ii) This expresses the suddenness in which it will occur.

Section 13.14   C. John 5:29

(a) 29 *And shall come forth; they that have done good, unto the resurrection of life; and they that have done evil, unto the resurrection of damnation.* (Joh 5:29 KJV)

- (i) Jesus also spoke of a resurrection of judgment.
- (ii) All will rise, but only those who have trusted Him for His atoning death are assured eternal life.

Section 13.15   D. I Corinthians 15:42-43 (A New Body)

(a) 42 *So also is the resurrection of the dead. It is sown in corruption; it is raised in incorruption: 43 It is sown in dishonour; it is raised in glory: it is sown in weakness; it is raised in power: 44 It is sown a natural body; it is raised a spiritual body. There is a natural body, and there is a spiritual body.* (1Co 15:42-44 KJV)

- (i) 1. It is imperishable, glorious and powerful, that is free from sickness or decay.

Section 13.16   E. Revelation 20:2-6

(a) *2 And he laid hold on the dragon, that old serpent, which is the Devil, and Satan, and bound him a thousand years, 3 And cast him into the bottomless pit, and shut him up, and set a seal upon him, that he should deceive the nations no more, till the thousand years should be fulfilled: and after that he must be loosed a little season. 4 And I saw thrones, and they sat upon them, and judgment was given unto them: and I saw the souls of them that were beheaded for the witness of Jesus, and for the word of God, and which had not worshipped the beast, neither his image, neither had received his mark upon their foreheads, or in their hands; and they lived and reigned with Christ a thousand years. 5 But the rest of the dead lived not again until the thousand years were finished. This is the first resurrection. 6 Blessed and holy is he that hath part in the first resurrection: on such the second death hath no power, but they shall be priests of God and of Christ, and shall reign with him a thousand years.* (Rev 20:2-6 KJV)

(i) The second coming of Christ will begin the thousand year reign with Christ over an earthly Kingdom.

(ii) During this period of time Satan will be bound and Saints reign with Christ before the last judgment.

Section 13.17   F. Revelation 21

(a) And I saw a new heaven and a new earth: for the first heaven and the first earth were passed away; and there was no more sea. 2 And I John saw the holy city, new Jerusalem, coming down from God out of heaven, prepared as a bride adorned for her husband. 3 And I heard a great voice out of heaven saying, Behold, the tabernacle of God is with men, and he will dwell with them, and they shall be his people, and God himself shall be with them, and be their God. 4 And God shall wipe away all tears from their eyes; and there shall be no more death, neither sorrow, nor crying, neither shall there be any more pain: for the former things are passed away. 5 And he that sat upon the throne said, Behold, I make all things new. And he said unto me, Write: for these words are true and faithful. 6 And he said unto me, It is done. I am Alpha and Omega, the beginning and the end. I will give unto him that is athirst of the fountain of the water of life freely. 7 He that overcometh shall inherit all things; and I will be his God, and he shall be my son. 8 But the fearful, and unbelieving, and the abominable, and murderers, and whoremongers, and sorcerers, and idolaters, and all liars, shall have their part in the lake which burneth with fire and brimstone: which is the second death. 9 And there came unto me one of the seven angels which had the seven vials full of the seven last plagues, and talked with me, saying, Come hither, I will shew thee the bride, the Lamb's wife. 10 And he carried me away in the spirit to a great and high mountain, and shewed me that great city, the holy Jerusalem, descending out of heaven from God, 11 Having the glory of God: and her light was like unto a stone most precious, even like a jasper stone, clear as crystal; 12 And had a wall great and high, and had twelve gates, and at the gates twelve angels, and names written thereon, which are the names of the twelve tribes of the children of Israel: 13 On the east three gates; on the north three gates; on the south three gates; and on the west three gates. 14 And the wall of the city had twelve foundations, and in them the names of the twelve apostles of the Lamb. 15 And he that talked with me had a golden reed to measure the city, and the gates thereof, and *the wall thereof. 16 And the city lieth foursquare, and the length is as large as the breadth: and he measured the city with the reed, twelve thousand furlongs. The length and the breadth and the height of it are equal. 17 And he measured the wall thereof, an hundred and forty and four cubits, according to the measure of a man, that is, of the angel. 18 And the building of the wall of it was of jasper: and the city was pure gold, like unto clear glass. 19 And the foundations of the wall of the city were garnished with all manner of precious stones. The first foundation was jasper; the second, sapphire; the third, a chalcedony; the fourth, an emerald; 20 The fifth, sardonyx; the sixth, sardius; the seventh, chrysolite; the eighth, beryl; the ninth, a topaz; the tenth, a chrysoprasus; the eleventh, a jacinth; the twelfth, an amethyst. 21 And the twelve gates were twelve pearls; every several gate was of one pearl: and the street of the city was pure gold, as it were transparent glass. 22 And I saw no temple therein: for the Lord God Almighty and the Lamb are the temple of it. 23 And the city had no need of the sun, neither of the moon, to shine in it: for the glory of God did lighten it, and the Lamb is the light thereof. 24 And the nations of them which are saved shall walk in the light of it: and the kings of the earth do bring their glory and honour into it. 25 And the gates of it shall not be shut at all by day: for there shall be no night there. 26 And they shall bring the glory and honour of the nations into it. 27 And there shall in no wise enter into it any thing that defileth, neither whatsoever worketh abomination, or maketh a lie: but they which are written in the Lamb's book of life. (Rev 21:1-27 KJV)*

(i) 1. This Describes how all Christians will be like Christ and share in His glory.

Article XIV. In the Final Judgment

Section 14.01 A. Revelation 20:15

(a) 15 *And whosoever was not found written in the book of life was cast into the lake of fire. (Rev 20:15 KJV)*

    (i) 1. The great White Throne Judgment describes the judgment of the wicked dead.

Section 14.02 B. Basis or grounds for the final judgment.

1. James 2:17-18

(a) *18 Yea, a man may say, Thou hast faith, and I have works: shew me thy faith without thy works, and I will shew thee my faith by my works. (Jam 2:18 KJV)*

    (i) Faith if it has no works is dead.
    (ii) The works expressed here is man's actual relationship with God.

2. Revelation 20:14-15

(b) *14 And death and hell were cast into the lake of fire. This is the second death.*

(c) *15 And whosoever was not found written in the book of life was cast into the lake of fire. (Rev 20:14-15 KJV)*

    (i) The results of this final judgment will be eternal.
    (ii) All those not found in the Lambs Book of Life will be condemned to the lake of fire.

3. Revelation 20:7-10

(d) *7 And when the thousand years are expired, Satan shall be loosed out of his prison, 8 And shall go out to deceive the nations which are in the four quarters of the earth, Gog and Magog, to gather them together to battle: the number of whom is as the sand of the sea. 9 And they went up on the breadth of the earth, and compassed the camp of the saints about, and the beloved city: and fire came down from God out of heaven, and devoured them. 10 And the devil that deceived them was cast into the lake of fire and brimstone, where the beast and the false prophet are, and shall be tormented day and night for ever and ever. (Rev 20:7-10 KJV)*

    (i) Satan will be released from the bottomless pit.

(ii) He will rise against Christ, at which time Satan and his armies will be defeated by fire.

Section 14.03 C. Future of the wicked believers is described.

(a) Luke 13:25,28

(b) 25 When once the master of the house is risen up, and hath shut to the door, and ye begin to stand without, and to knock at the door, saying, Lord, Lord, open unto us; and he shall answer and say unto you, I know you not whence ye are: (Luk 13:25 KJV)

(c) 28 There shall be weeping and gnashing of teeth, when ye shall see Abraham, and Isaac, and Jacob, and all the prophets, in the kingdom of God, and you yourselves thrust out. (Luk 13:28 KJV)

(i) a. Separation from God.

(d) Revelation 14:10-11

(e) 10 The same shall drink of the wine of the wrath of God, which is poured out without mixture into the cup of his indignation; and he shall be tormented with fire and brimstone in the presence of the holy angels, and in the presence of the Lamb: 11 And the smoke of their torment ascendeth up for ever and ever: and they have no rest day nor night, who worship the beast and his image, and whosoever receiveth the mark of his name. (Rev 14:10-11 KJV)

(i) a. Everlasting torment.

Article XV. In the Final Judgment p2

Section 15.01   A. Matthew 25:46

(a) *46 And these shall go away into everlasting punishment: but the righteous into life eternal. (Mat 25:46 KJV)*

   (i) This is the future for the saints.
   (ii) Eternal Life.

Section 15.02   B. II Corinthians 4:17

(a) *17 For our light affliction, which is but for a moment, worketh for us a far more exceeding and eternal weight of glory; (2Co 4:17 KJV)*

   (i) 1. Heaven is a place of glory.

Section 15.03   C. Hebrews 4:9

(a) *9 There remaineth therefore a rest to the people of God. (Heb 4:9 KJV)*

   (i) A place of rest.
   (ii) A greater peace and well being waits in Heaven.

Section 15.04   D. I Corinthians 13:8-10

(a) *8 Charity never faileth: but whether there be prophecies, they shall fail; whether there be tongues, they shall cease; whether there be knowledge, it shall vanish away. 9 For we know in part, and we prophesy in part. 10 But when that which is perfect is come, then that which is in part shall be done away. (1Co 13:8-10 KJV)*

   (i) 1. Knowledge of fulfillment of prophecy

Section 15.05   E. Revelation 21:27

(a) 27 *And there shall in no wise enter into it any thing that defileth, neither whatsoever worketh abomination, or maketh a lie: but they which are written in the Lamb's book of life. (Rev 21:27 KJV)*

    (i) 1. Holiness – we have been called to holiness.

Section 15.06   F. Revelation 22:3

(a) *3 And there shall be no more curse: but the throne of God and of the Lamb shall be in it; and his servants shall serve him: (Rev 22:3 KJV)*

    (i) 1. We have been called to service to God which is an easy, light yoke and burden.

Section 15.07   G. Revelation 19:1

(a) *And after these things I heard a great voice of much people in heaven, saying, Alleluia; Salvation, and glory, and honour, and power, unto the Lord our God: (Rev 19:1 KJV)*

    (i) 1. We will be able to worship God in truth and with a pure and holy heart.

Section 15.08   H. Revelation 21:3

(a) *3 And I heard a great voice out of heaven saying, Behold, the tabernacle of God is with men, and he will dwell with them, and they shall be his people, and God himself shall be with them, and be their God. (Rev 21:3 KJV)*

    (i) Communion with God.
    (ii) This is our number one goal.

Article XVI.   In a New Heaven and a New Earth

Section 16.01   A. Psalm 102:25, 26

(a) 25 *Of old hast thou laid the foundation of the earth: and the heavens are the work of thy hands. 26 They shall perish, but thou shalt endure: yea, all of them shall wax old like a garment; as a vesture shalt thou change them, and they shall be changed: (Psa 102:25-26 KJV)*

- (i) Heaven and Earth will have a new beginning.
- (ii) This will be a place were only the righteous will be.
- (iii) II Peter 3:10, 13

Section 16.02   B. Isaiah 65:17

(a) *17 For, behold, I create new heavens and a new earth: and the former shall not be remembered, nor come into mind. (Isa 65:17 KJV)*

- (i) This will take place at the end of the millennium after all rebellion is put down on Earth.
- (ii) All enemies are destroyed and God's rule is final.

Section 16.03   C. Isaiah 66:22, 23

(a) *22 For as the new heavens and the new earth, which I will make, shall remain before me, saith the LORD, so shall your seed and your name remain. 23 And it shall come to pass, that from one new moon to another, and from one sabbath to another, shall all flesh come to worship before me, saith the LORD. (Isa 66:22-23 KJV)*

- (i) The old universe will be marvelously regenerated.
- (ii) Those with resurrection bodies will dwell with their God in a regenerated universe.

Section 16.04   D. Acts 3:19

(a) *19 Repent ye therefore, and be converted, that your sins may be blotted out, when the times of refreshing shall come from the presence of the Lord; (Act 3:19 KJV)*

(i) This will be a place were eternal happiness will be found.
(ii) That means no more sadness, sorrow, pain or suffering.

Section 16.05   B. Genesis 3:19

(a) *19 In the sweat of thy face shalt thou eat bread, till thou return unto the ground; for out of it wast thou taken: for dust thou art, and unto dust shalt thou return. (Gen 3:19 KJV)*

(i) No more pain, no death, no thorns but peace.
(ii) This only means comfort and no reason to be anxious about anything.

Section 16.06   C. Romans 8:17

(a) *17 And if children, then heirs; heirs of God, and joint-heirs with Christ; if so be that we suffer with him, that we may be also glorified together. (Rom 8:17 KJV)*

(i) We will inherit all things.
(ii) We will be rich in the Lord.

Section 16.07   D. I John 3:1-2

(a) *Behold, what manner of love the Father hath bestowed upon us, that we should be called the sons of God: therefore the world knoweth us not, because it knew him not. 2 Beloved, now are we the sons of God, and it doth not yet appear what we shall be: but we know that, when he shall appear, we shall be like him; for we shall see him as he is. (1Jo 3:1-2 KJV)*

(i) Eternal sonship.

Article XVII.   II. Events of New Heaven and Earth
Section 17.01   Philippians 2:10-11

(a) *10 That at the name of Jesus every knee should bow, of things in heaven, and things in earth, and things under the earth; 11 And that every tongue should confess that Jesus Christ is Lord, to the glory of God the Father. (Phi 2:10-11 KJV)*

- (i) Confession of all creation.
- (ii) All creation will bow in submission to Christ as King.

Section 17.02 Ephesians 2:7, 3:11, 21

(a) *7 That in the ages to come he might shew the exceeding riches of his grace in his kindness toward us through Christ Jesus. (Eph 2:7 KJV)*

(b) *11 According to the eternal purpose which he purposed in Christ Jesus our Lord: (Eph 3:11 KJV)*

(c) *21 Unto him be glory in the church by Christ Jesus throughout all ages, world without end. Amen. (Eph 3:21-1 KJV)*

- (i) Eternal ages begin.
- (ii) All saints will forever demonstrate the over flowing wealth of God's grace.

Printed in Great Britain
by Amazon